EARS

Santa Fe Writers Group

John Muir Publications
Santa Fe, New Mexico

Special thanks to Mary Colleen McNamara, Ph.D., Department of Biology, Albuquerque Technical-Vocational Institute, Albuquerque, New Mexico

Santa Fe Writers Group:
Sharon Moscinski, research and writing
Donald E. Fineberg
A. S. Gintzler
Miriam Sagan
Leda Silver

John Muir Publications, P.O. Box 613, Santa Fe, New Mexico 87504
© 1993 by John Muir Publications

Printed in the United States of America
Printed on recycled paper

First edition. First printing September 1993
        First TWG printing September 1993

Library of Congress Cataloging-in-Publication Data
Bizarre & beautiful ears / Santa Fe Writers Group.
        p. cm.
    Includes index.
    Summary: Describes the ears and sense of hearing of such diverse animals as the beetle, dolphin, and snake.
ISBN 1-56261-122-4 : $14.95
1. Hearing—Juvenile literature. 2. Ears—Juvenile literature. 3. Physiology—Comparative—Juvenile literature.
[1. Hearing. 2. Senses and sensation. 3. Ears. 4. Animals—Physiology.]
I. Santa Fe Writers Group. II. Title: Bizarre and beautiful ears.
QP462.2.B59 1993
591.1'825—dc20   93-19592
                                                              CIP
                                                              AC

Logo/Interior Design: Ken Wilson
Illustrations: Chris Brigman
Typography: Ken Wilson
Printer: Guynes Printing Company

Distributed to the book trade by
W. W. Norton & Co., Inc.
500 Fifth Ave.
New York, New York 10110

Distributed to the education market by
The Wright Group
19201 120th Avenue NE
Bothell, WA 98011

Cover photo, African serval, Animals Animals © Robert Pearcy
Back cover photo, Cape fur seal, Animals Animals © Anthony Bannister

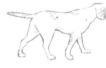

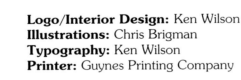

Introduction

All animals on the planet, including humans, understand the world around them by using sensory organs. The senses we know the most about are sight, smell, taste, touch, and hearing. Animals use these senses to avoid predators, to find mates, food, and shelter, and to entertain themselves. Some people believe that animals, including humans, use other, less-understood senses as well. Have you ever had a "hunch" about something that proved to be true? Maybe you were using a sense other than one of the five mentioned above.

One of the most important senses in the animal kingdom is hearing. Ears and other hearing organs allow creatures to perceive each other's **acoustic signals**, sounds meant to communicate. Mosquitoes buzz, dolphins click, foxes growl and peep, monkeys scream and chatter—and humans make all kinds of noise! We talk with each other, laugh, sing, whisper, hoot, and holler. In fact, the more acoustic signals a type of animal makes, the more sensitive its hearing and complex its hearing organs. That's because we have to understand, and be understood by, members of our own species.

Hearing also plays an important role in our safety. We can hear the honk of a car horn, or someone yelling "Watch out!" In the same way, animals warn each other with sounds. Hearing also brings pleasure. We can enjoy music, the lap of ocean waves, the sound of a good belly laugh, wind blowing through treetops, or the hard crack of bat meeting ball and the stadium filling with cheers.

Bizarre and Beautiful Ears takes you on a tour of the sense of hearing in the animal world. But before we listen in on the twenty animals featured in this book, let's cover the basics of hearing.

The disk-shaped membranes behind the frog's eyes collect sound.

The dog has a complicated ear made up of three parts: the outer ear, the middle ear, and the inner ear.

Papillon dog

GOOD VIBRATIONS

Sound is made of **vibrations** produced by movement. The movement can be as slight as a ladybug crawling on a blade of grass or as large as a hurricane ripping through a town. These vibrations travel in **waves**. Though light can travel through a vacuum like outer space, sound cannot. It needs a medium to travel through. Usually that medium is air, water, or earth.

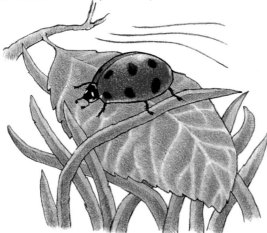

Sound waves are vibrations produced by movement, no matter how small.

The average human speaking voice measures around 60 decibels. A rock band plays at over 120 decibels. Sounds above 140 decibels, such as jet planes taking off, can be painful to your ears, and possibly even injure them.

Our sense of hearing helps us communicate with each other and avoid danger. It is also our key to the world of beautiful sounds.

Sounds can have different pitches; they can be high or low or somewhere in between. Pitch is determined by the **frequency** of the sound waves—the number of vibrations they produce in a second. A high-frequency sound, such as fingernails scraping a blackboard, has a high pitch. A low-frequency sound—thunder, for example—has a low pitch. Frequency is measured in **hertz**. The normal range for humans is 20 to 20,000 hertz. Bats, cats, dogs, and other animals can hear sounds of far higher frequency, called **ultrasound**. In fact, bats produce and hear high-pitched ultrasound that measures over 100,000 hertz! Sounds also vary in volume—how loud or soft they are. This is called **intensity** and is measured in **decibels**.

AN AUDITORY ASSORTMENT

Not all ears are alike—far from it. Mammals' ears are on the sides or the tops of their heads. But crickets' ears are on their legs, and moths' ears are under their wings! Some ears are very simple while others, like our own, are complex organs.

Some ears are big and floppy, others are small and pointy. But if they're made of skin, you know they belong to a mammal. Land mammals are the only animals with fleshy outer ears, called **pinnae**. You've probably seen rabbits prick up their tall ears when

BALANCING ACT

Have you *ever* spun yourself around and around until you collapsed dizzily to the floor? What you did was upset your **balance**. To be exact, you sent scrambled messages to your brain, so it was unable to make the necessary adjustments that keep you upright.

Structures in the inner ear gather balance-sensing information and send it to the brain. This is why an injury to your ear can sometimes make you feel "woozy" or unsteady on your feet. Some organs in your ear work to maintain balance while you are still—sitting down, for example. These are called the **saccule** and **utricle**. The **semicircular canals** tell your brain when you are about to lose your balance during movement. If you're about to fall off your bicycle, for example, this organ will alert your brain so it can tell the right muscles to save you from toppling over.

Your eyes and special cells in the soles of your feet and the joints of your arms and legs also help keep you right-side-up.

In many animals, ears serve not only to hear but to help maintain balance.

they're listening, and lay them down flat when they're munching on grass. Humans cannot move their pinnae like this to channel sound into the ear, but some people *can* contract their ear muscles—otherwise known as "wiggling" their ears.

Birds and most reptiles and marine mammals have ear slits on the sides of their head. This ear slit is called the **auditory canal**. Fish do not have any outer ears at all, not even ear slits. They pick up sound vibrations through their skin and pass it on to their inner ears.

The Path of Sound

Despite all of these different kinds of ears, there are some common elements to the sense of hearing. First, sound waves enter the ear and hit the **eardrum**, or **tympanic membrane**. (Animals with no outer ears sense sound waves through bone or tissue.) The eardrum passes the sound waves to the **middle** and **inner ear**, where they are changed into electrical nerve signals that are sent to the brain. The brain then perceives (understands) these signals as sound.

This book can only give you a glimpse of all the fascinating things there are to learn about ears and hearing. But it will introduce you to many of the interesting ways animals relate to their environment and to each other. We hope this book sparks you to learn more about the sense of hearing. You'll find a list of suggested reading at the end. If you want to review a term (*sound wave*, for example), or if you come across a word you don't understand (what's *ultrasound*?), turn to the glossarized index at the back. But first, let's enter the bizarre and beautiful world of ears.

Moths

(Order: Lepidoptera)

We don't usually expect ears to grow out of the chest, but that's where moths' ears are: just below the second pair of wings. The moth has the simplest known auditory (hearing) system in the animal kingdom. Its primitive "ears" are made up of a tympanic membrane (its "eardrum") and two acoustic sensory cells. One of these cells is more sensitive than the other. Together they are tuned to pick up ultrasound and are especially alert to the calls of bats. Why bats? Because these flying mammals are the moth's main predator. Humans cannot hear the high-pitched sounds that bats make when they chirp, but moths can. They can even tell how far away a bat is.

Imagine if you had two wings flapping up and down over your ears. It might make it difficult to hear. The same goes for moths. They hear much better when their wings are on the upstroke, exposing the tympanic membrane. With its two "ears," the moth can listen in different directions. And it can hear both loud and soft sounds. If a bat's cries are faint and far away, the moth will turn and fly in the opposite direction. But if the bat is gaining fast, the moth will respond with escape tactics. The fleeing moth might make loops in the air, or fold its wings and drop suddenly to the ground. The result is an aerial battle in which the moth still has a chance for survival.

MUSICAL MOTHS

People used to think that moths were tone-deaf, but a summer dinner party suggested otherwise. When a guest ran his wet finger around the rim of a glass, making a ringing sound, dozens of moths dropped to the ground from where they had been fluttering around paper lanterns. The professor who was giving the party was intrigued and began to research moths. Scientists soon discovered that moths react to many musical sounds.

To escape a bat, some moths make loops in the air. Others fold their wings and drop to the ground.

Pericopid moth, above and facing page

MOSQUITOES

(Family: Culicidae)

Hardly anything is more annoying than a mosquito's buzzing—except maybe its itchy bite. But the mosquito's buzz serves a purpose in the insect world, as does its ability to hear. Mosquitoes don't have ears. Like many insects, they use thread-like filaments called hair sensilla to listen. These are lightly hinged to the insect's two antennae and can move freely in the breeze. They also move to low-frequency sounds.

When female mosquitoes fly, the beating of their wings produces a low-frequency sound that is irresistible to male mosquitoes. The female mosquito has less developed hearing since it plays no important role in her survival. Just as moths' ears are especially sensitive to one thing—the sounds made by their bat predators—the mosquito's sense of hearing also serves a limited purpose, to find a mate.

The mosquito's hair sensilla pick up certain sounds, but the mosquito may not know their meaning. For example, male mosquitoes will flock to a tuning fork if it is vibrating at the pitch made by the female's wings. Male mosquitoes can even be lured to an electric generator! At one new power station, electricians couldn't figure out why the brand new generators kept breaking down. Finally, they discovered that the generators were jammed with thousands of male mosquitoes that responded to the electric hum. The electricians solved their problem by changing the speed of the generators so they would no longer be mistaken for female mosquitoes!

HARD OF HEARING

The female mosquito beats her wings 500 times a second! The male is sensitive enough to locate a female 8 feet (about 2.5 meters) away. But if a gummy substance is placed on the male's antennae, he will no longer pay any attention to the female. It's as if he were wearing ear plugs!

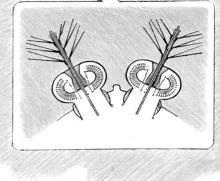

Like many insects, mosquitoes hear with thread-like filaments called hair sensilla attached to their antennae.

Black salt marsh mosquito, facing page

Crickets

(Family: Gryllidae)

Moth's have ears beneath their wings. Mosquitoes listen with antennae on top of their head, and crickets ears' are on their front legs. Their hearing is directional, which means they have to point their ears at the sound itself. Imagine listening to a conversation by pointing your knees towards the speaker!

The cricket's ears, like the ears of other insects, are very simple, just an eardrum and nerves that pick up sound vibration. It is a basic system, yet many insects can hear beyond the normal range for human ears.

In the cricket world, only the males sing. Crickets produce their song by rubbing parts of their body together. The short-horned field cricket, for example, moves its back legs up and down. On the inside of each leg, there is a row of tiny teeth that scrapes against the forewing, creating the song. Some crickets sing by rubbing their forewings together.

Male crickets sing one song to attract the female cricket into the area, and a different one to court her once she's there. Sometimes a group of males sing together in a loud chorus, drawing several females to them. Interestingly, the song of one cricket species won't attract a female from another species. Two species of insects simply don't understand each other—it's as if one were speaking Spanish and the other Russian! Crickets also sing to drive away other males. This is especially true of the type of cricket who lives alone in a burrow and sings to defend its territory.

Nisitrus cricket

SONG OF LIFE

The field grasshopper, a cousin of the cricket, has a song for *every* important occasion—and if you're a grasshopper, there are only three. The "calling song" is a long melody designed to attract the female. If two males meet, they burst into the "rival's song." This short tune has strong aggressive accents. If a female joins them, they begin chirping the "courting song."

EAR

The cricket's simple ears are on its front legs.

Saddle-backed bush cricket, facing page

10

DrUmFiSh

(Equetus punctatus)

How did the drum fish get its name? From its peculiar grunting, which sounds like a drumbeat. The drum fish has no vocal organs like mammals and birds. It produces its "drumbeat" by rapidly contracting and expanding muscles to vibrate its air bladder. (This motion can be as fast as 24 times per second!) The air bladder is a gas-filled sac in the abdominal (belly) cavity, between the fish's spine and intestines. It helps keep the fish at the ocean depth it prefers. When the walls of the air bladder vibrate, the sound resonates and is projected out into the water.

Drum fishes, like all fishes, lack an outer ear. So how do they hear each other? They pick up sound vibrations through the sides of their bodies and collect them with their air bladders. The air bladder then passes the sound vibrations on to four small structures (called the Weberian apparatus) in the fish's middle ear. From there, the vibrations travel to the fish's inner ear, or labyrinth. (It's called a labyrinth because it resembles a maze.) Next, the fluids in the labyrinth jiggle. Tiny hair cells in the labyrinth pick up the jiggle and flash signals to the fish's brain.

The middle and inner ears of people and fish are alike in many ways. The air bladder of the fish's middle ear is similar to the eardrum in mammals. The fish's Weberian apparatus is similar to four tiny bones in your own ear. The fluids in the inner ears of fish and humans are pretty much the same, too.

A FISHY SOUND

Are fish quiet? Not at all. The reason we do not hear their acoustic signals is that most fish noises are reflected back from the surface and stay underwater. But advances in the science of underwater bioacoustics (the sounds made by living things) reveal a wide variety of sounds produced by fish. Did you know that, in general, ocean fish hear mainly low notes, and freshwater fish hear mainly high notes?

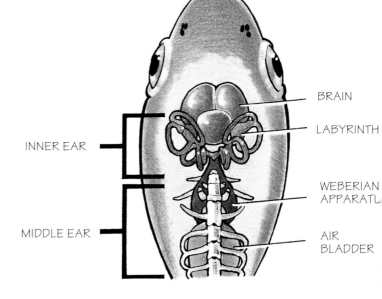

Many fishes, including the drum fish, collect sound vibrations with their air bladder.

Spotted drum fish, above and facing page

FROGS

(Order: Salientia)

When it comes to croaking, frogs are the experts. Frog calls consist of both low- and high-frequency vibrations that resonate like human vowel sounds. Frogs make many kinds of calls: mating calls, warning and distress calls, calls of territory ownership, and calls in response to other calls. Often, these have harmonic structures that remind us of music. Have you ever heard a frog chorus in full swing? Step on a twig or make some slight noise and they'll all fall silent. Frogs' sensitive ears alert them to potential danger.

Frogs have no outer ear like we do to capture and direct sound to the inner ear. If you look closely behind a frog's eyes, you'll see two round disks. These are the frog's tympanic membranes, the animal's eardrums. When sounds hit the tightly stretched membrane, it jiggles and passes the vibrations along a small bone to the inner ear labyrinth. This labyrinth is a system of sacs and canals that passes vibrations on to the auditory nerves. In turn, these nerves pass impulses to the frog's brain, which understands the impulses as sound.

Frogs need their ears for more than hearing. The inner ear labyrinth maintains a frog's equilibrium, or balance. If the labyrinth is damaged, a frog loses its ability to sit upright, to swim, or to coordinate its leg movements. Without their ears, frogs would dive, dip, and dunk dizzily.

European tree frog

FROM LUNG TO DRUM

Frogs start out as fish-like tadpoles that live in water. In a process called metamorphosis, they grow legs, absorb their tails, and undergo other changes to become amphibious frogs. Amphibians are animals that are able to live both in and out of water. Tadpoles' ears change, too. Frogs have eardrums to hear on dry land, but tadpoles don't. Instead, tadpoles pick up vibrations with their lungs.

Tadpoles don't develop ears until they're adult frogs. Until then, they "hear" with their lungs.

Giant tree frog, facing page

SNakes

(Order: Squamata)

A snake charmer plays his flute as a cobra rises from its basket, swaying to the music—or so it seems. Is the snake really "charmed" by the music? Can the snake even hear the haunting melody it seems to dance to?

The answer is no. Snakes have neither outer ears nor middle ear cavities. But they aren't deaf. Their hearing is quite good for detecting low-frequency sounds carried through ground vibrations. Thudding footsteps, for instance, vibrate through the ground and are picked up by a snake's jaw bones, then carried through other bones to the inner ear. The inner ear is a system of tubes which are filled with a fluid. The fluid passes vibrations to a duct called a cochlea. It is shaped like a snail's shell and named after the Greek word for snail. There, tiny hair cells pick up the vibrations, turn them into a signal the brain can understand, then send them to the brain which interprets the vibrations as sound.

A researcher named Colonel Wells tested cobras' response to noise. He blindfolded the snakes, then walked nearby, causing the ground to vibrate. The snakes reared up, spread their hoods, and faced the direction of his footsteps. When he stood still and blew a bugle, the snakes didn't react at all! But some snakes *do* react to some airborne sounds. Does this mean that cobras can hear the music of snake charmers after all?

No. "Charmed" cobras are actually responding to the moving arms and legs of their charmers—which they *see* with their eyes.

Rough green snake

SNAKES ON LAND

Snakes and other reptiles were the first vertebrates (animals with backbones) to lay their eggs on land. They were an important part of animals' evolution from water to land. In the inner ear of snakes and other reptiles are similarities to the ears of humans and other mammals.

Snakes "hear" ground vibrations, such as footsteps and the movement of prey, through their jaw bones.

Yellow rat snake, facing page

Kangaroo Rats

(Genera *Dipodomys* and *Microdipodops*)

The kangaroo rat is a small nocturnal rodent that lives in desert areas. Both the rattlesnake and the owl like to dine on the kangaroo rat. The rattlesnake has the unique ability to sense the heat given off by warm-blooded prey such as the kangaroo rat. And the owl has keen vision and spectacular hearing, more precise than radar itself. How can the kangaroo rat possibly escape from these powerful predators?

By using its extra-sensitive hearing, that's how. The rodent's ears not only hear but actually amplify (make louder) sounds such as that of an owl's beating wings. Kangaroo rats can even detect the sound of an owl gliding, its wings outspread. (Humans can hear this soundless flight only when it is amplified electronically.)

Just as the owl is about to snatch up the kangaroo rat in its sharp talons, the rodent leaps into the air like the kangaroo it is named after. It can jump at least a foot away from where the owl strikes, empty-clawed.

Just before it strikes, a rattlesnake makes a sound—often too faint for humans to hear. The sound may be a rattle or a hiss or just the glide of scales along the ground. But the kangaroo rat hears the snake clearly, and once again makes a leap to safety.

Chisel-toothed kangaroo rat

The kangaroo rat leaps to safety thanks to its ability to hear the faint sound a rattlesnake makes before it strikes.

Desert kangaroo rat, facing page

MIDDLE EAR FOR LOW RANGE

The ear of the kangaroo rat is unusual. Its middle ear cavity is much bigger than in other animals its size. Its large middle ear enables the kangaroo rat to hear low-frequency sound waves. And that is just the range it needs to detect the rattlesnake's slither or the owl's whoosh of wings.

18

Foxes

(Genus: *Vulpes*)

Y ou would hear nothing, but fox ears are so sensitive they can hear the high-pitched squeak of insect larvae in the ground. The bat-eared fox of southwest Africa claws the ground at night, hunting for termites and dung beetle larvae. Sound tasty? To the bat-eared fox, there is nothing tastier. Insects are the main ingredient of its diet.

Foxes have a keen sense of hearing, which they use for listening to each other, as well as to insects. Pups listen for their parents' call. When they hear the high whistling sound of the adult foxes, the pups leave their snug underground burrow to join their parents. When foxes groom each other, they make a satisfied peeping sound. When bat-eared foxes "argue" over food, they growl at each other, sounding a lot like small dogs. When a fox is cornered or captured by predators or human hunters, it yelps and woofs.

The way a fox holds its ears reflects what it is doing and how it feels. For example, a fox points its ears forward when it is alert and listening. When startled or distressed, the ears lie down flat against the head, similar to a hissing cat. (By the way, foxes are related to dogs and wolves, not cats, as many people think.) And if a fox is threatened, it lays its ears down and turns the black insides of the ears forward, trying to look fierce.

Cape fox

HOT AND COLD EARS

The fennec fox of north Africa and the bat-eared fox of southwest Africa have tall, dramatic ears. These ears have a large surface area with many blood vessels that disperse heat. This helps the foxes endure the scorching temperature of their desert habitat (living space). The arctic fox lives in an extremely cold region. It has to keep its body heat inside. To survive the freezing temperatures, the fox exposes less surface area. What size ears do you suppose the arctic fox has? You guessed it: very small ones.

Once the fox hears the high-pitched squeak of insect larvae, it claws the ground in search of a snack.

Fennec fox, facing page

BATS

(Order: Chiroptera)

Bennett's spear-nosed bat

Blind as a bat? Actually, bats *see* better than people do—but they "*see*" with their ears! A bat can zero in on a moth and snatch it out of thin air at 60 miles an hour on a pitch black night, blindfolded. Wow! How? Bats form complex mental pictures of their surroundings by emitting short bursts of sound that bounce off objects and back to their ears. These bouncing sounds are known as echoes, and this method of "seeing" is called echolocation. There are more than 900 species of bats worldwide, but it is the insect-eating bats who are the champs of echolocation. (Their eyes are so weak that they can barely tell whether it's day or night.)

It all starts in the bat's throat, where the animal produces high-frequency sounds that shoot out through its mouth or nose, sometimes both. The bat's outer ears (pinnae) are very flexible and highly sensitive. They listen carefully to the echoes of their squeaks and can tell how far away an object is by how long it takes for the echo to return. Bats can detect insects up to 18 feet (about 5.5 meters) away. Bats' super-sensitive ears also can determine the shape of an insect or other object by the way the sound has changed when it comes back as an echo.

Although bats make many noises that humans can hear, we can't detect the ultrasonic beeps they use for echolocation. Ultrasound is very high-frequency sound, way beyond the range humans can hear. (*Ultra* means high.) So, when you see a bat swooping after moths on a summer night, you can be sure they're beeping and squeaking like mad—even though you can't hear a thing.

ANTENNAE EARS

A lively pair of ears is essential in echo-location. Bats can move their pinnae (outer ears) very rapidly—as fast as six times per second—while using them as echo receivers. Horseshoe bats can move each ear in different directions, but most bats move both ears in the same direction.

Bats use echolocation to hunt moths, one of their favorite foods.

Long-eared bat, facing page

SHrews

(Genus: *Sorex*)

These small mammals live in underground tunnel systems, often along rivers or wet meadows. Their ears vary somewhat depending on their habitat. For example, those in cooler climates have hairy ears for warmth, while those in tropical areas have naked ears.

Shrews are a "talkative" bunch. They use a variety of sounds to communicate with each other. If a baby shrew falls out of its tunnel nest or is hungry, it will bark until its mother appears. Mothers and infants also whisper to each other, which may serve as their way of recognizing each other.

Some shrews shriek when they are startled, probably to scare off predators. Shrews "talk" three different ways: they hiss through their nose, click with their tongue, and vocalize from their larynx, the vocal organ in the throat. (To vocalize means to make sound with vocal organs, in contrast to making sound by, say, clapping your hands.)

The shrew's high-pitched twitter serves a special purpose. Some of these sounds are actually ultrasonic (very high-frequency) and work by echolocation to help the shrew find its way around, especially in the dim light or darkness of its tunnel world. The shrew bounces its own voice off surrounding obstacles and, through the returning "echo," gets a clearer picture of its environment.

Shrews also use hearing to hunt. When a shrew hears a rustling noise, it immediately leaps to investigate. Shrews sniff about in their burrows or through the undergrowth until they find the insect larvae they like to munch on. But while they may be bold with small critters like insect larvae, shrews are generally very cautious. Before leaving its burrow, the shrew sticks out its snout. It is smelling for danger but also clicking and whistling, using echolocation to determine whether it's safe to come out.

Elephant shrew

NOT JUST FOR BATS

Scientists are discovering that more and more animals use echolocation. A variety of mammals are sensitive to ultrasound, including rats, hamsters, dormice, and marmosets. The long, twitching whiskers and large, flexible pinnae (outer ears) of these animals help them with echolocation by effectively collecting sound.

The shrew hears in part through echolocation, which it uses to hunt.

Common tree shrew, facing page

Songbirds

(Suborder: Passeres)

Songbirds and people hear pretty much the same musical notes. Yet, in a way, birds have hearing superior to ours. With very rapid notes, they can distinguish pitch (how high or low a sound is) better than we can. And birds can hear and respond to a song about ten times faster than humans. Their eardrums are also stronger. Loud and continuous noise can damage mammals' ears, but it seems impossible to deafen birds this way.

Take a look at the songbirds' ears. Where are they? Mostly hidden. The middle and inner ears of birds are very similar to those of mammals. But instead of the fleshy outer ears we have, birds have a tiny opening covered with feathers on either side of their head. No big, protruding ears means a sleeker body line for flight.

Hearing is the most important sense for birds. They can hear and respond to songs and calls of their own species, as well as many other noises. For the most part, songs claim territory, like a musical "No Trespassing Allowed!" sign. Other songs are used for courtship ("Be my mate!"), or alarm ("Predator nearby!"), or finding food ("Look! Worms!"). Some species can mimic other birds and even humans. Parrots, budgies, mynahs, magpies, crows, and starlings are famous for imitating the human voice and for whistling. The ability to mimic relies on acute and selective hearing.

Blue jay

BABY TALK

When newly hatched birds were kept in sound-proof cages until a certain age, they could still produce the sounds of their species and answer other birds' sounds correctly. This ability is instinctive, rather than learned. Can a human baby understand human speech if no one speaks to it and it never hears people talk? No. Every child learns from hearing others speak.

Bird songs often serve to warn others that a predator lurks nearby.

Cardinal, facing page

Dogs

(Canis familiaris)

ogs can hear a thunderstorm miles off. They can detect approaching visitors well before they knock on the door. They can hear small animals scurrying through brambles a considerable distance away. Many dogs can even distinguish the sound of their owner's car from the sound of other cars! These feats are possible because dogs have an extraordinarily acute sense of hearing.

Dog ears come in all shapes and sizes—pointy, shaped like tear drops, tulip-shaped, and just plain floppy. All forms of dog ears can hear far better than humans. Breeds with erect ears, like German shepherds and foxhounds, can hear best of all. When these pointy-eared pooches hear a noise, they prick up their ears and cock their heads to one side to locate the direction of the sound. Their wide-open ears act as effective antennae that can be turned to zero in on faint sounds. Dogs with floppy ears have a less acute sense of hearing since their ear flaps muffle incoming sound waves.

But whatever the shape and size of their ears, dogs hear sounds that are not only too distant for humans to hear, but also those that are too high in frequency. Dogs will respond to a pitch of 30,000 hertz, whereas very few humans hear sounds above 20,000 hertz. (Remember, frequency is measured in hertz.) These facts help explain the mysterious "silent" dog whistle. Puff into one of these, and you will hear nothing. Your dog, however, will hear a piercing blast over a half a mile away!

EAR SERVICE

Most people are familiar with guide dogs for the blind, but few know about dogs for the deaf, called hearing ear dogs. These dogs are trained to be helpers and companions to deaf people. Hearing ear dogs alert their owners when alarm clocks go off, doorbells ring, oven timers buzz, and tea kettles whistle. They even let deaf parents know when their baby is crying. Hearing ear dogs make it possible for deaf people to live more worry-free, independent lives.

All dogs have keen hearing, but breeds with pointy ears hear best of all.

Shetland sheepdog, facing page

Dolphins

(Delphinus delphis)

Like bats, these intelligent aquatic mammals use echolocation to interpret sound and orient themselves to their surroundings. Even humans use echolocation—an electronic version, that is, called sonar, for Sound Navigation Ranging. But dolphins do it naturally; they send out a series of clicks or ticking noises that travel through the water and then bounce off objects as echoes. The time it takes for an echo to return and the direction the echo comes from tell the dolphin the object's location.

Dolphins listen for these sounds with more than just their ears, which appear as tiny slits on either side of the head. Dolphins also use their lower jaws to receive sound and direct it to the inner ear and nerve centers. The lower jaw for hearing? Yes, because it is filled with an oily substance perfect for conducting vibrations. In one experiment, a blindfolded dolphin located an underwater sound transmitter, then placed its jaw against the speaker and kept it there for a long time—listening with its jaw, not its ears!

While cruising underwater, dolphins scan their general surroundings by sending out low frequencies, or wavelengths, of sound. Echoes from these sounds give dolphins "the big picture" of their environment. When zeroing in on an object, they transmit high frequencies of clicking sounds—as many as several hundred per second!—for a clearer, more accurate picture. Researchers are studying dolphins in the hope of developing electronic sonar and radar devices to help sightless people to "see."

SAY WHAT?

Do dolphins talk? According to some zoologists (scientists who study animals), dolphins communicate with each other using sequences of clicks, squeaks, whines, and other sounds. While traveling in schools, they may stop and have "discussions" about their surroundings and the best route to take around obstacles.

Dolphins send out scouts to explore an area and report back to the group.

Bottle-nosed dolphin, above and facing page

OILbirds

(Steatornis caripensis)

Deep inside the pitch black caverns of the South American jungle lives a peculiar creature called an oilbird. The oilbird's claim to fame is that it is one of the only birds in the entire world that uses echolocation—and it is a good thing that it does! The caves that the oilbird inhabits are so dark that eyesight is useless. The oilbird must depend solely on echolocation to navigate itself through the long, rocky passages of its cave home.

As the oilbird swoops through its unlit cave, it emits a series of low-frequency sounds, which humans hear as clicks. The sound waves of these "clicks" ricochet off nearby objects back to the bird's ears. The oilbird can then detect the presence of dangerous obstacles by analyzing the time delay between the initial "clicks" and the returning echoes. The longer the time delay, the farther away the object. But if the echoes return very quickly—look out! It means an obstacle is straight ahead, and the oilbird must hastily whoosh in the opposite direction to avoid a head-on collision.

Unlike bats, oilbirds do not use echolocation to find food. Rather, once out in the moonlit jungle, these nocturnal creatures rely on their keen sense of vision to locate the fruit they feed on. Echolocation is mostly helpful to oilbirds because it enables them to roost and nest in the total darkness of caves.

FRUGIVOROUS FEATHERED FRIENDS

The oilbird's snazzy sonar does more than enable them to navigate through the dark caves in which they live. It is also the reason they can be frugivorous (meaning they eat only fruit). Most birds cannot feed their young fruit because on such a diet nestlings grow more slowly and so are exposed to predators for a longer period of time. However, oilbirds can take full advantage of the abundant jungle fruit supply because their young are nestled in the high crevices inside caves, safe from predators.

Oilbirds use echolocation to navigate in the dark caves where they build their nests.

Oilbird, above and facing page

Monkeys

(Order: Primata)

Proboscis monkey

onkeys' ears aren't very different from other mammals' ears. In general, they have excellent hearing. Monkeys make and understand complex acoustic signals: they scream, chatter, hoot, and grunt to communicate with each other. Like humans, monkeys are sociable animals. They live in tight-knit groups and must listen to and understand each other to survive.

Infant monkeys spend a long time with their mothers learning the many sounds used by their species. Yet even very young monkeys have calls to get attention or show distress. The infant vervet (or green monkey) has at least five distress calls when separated from its mother. The calls vary in frequency (remember low frequency and high frequency?) and intensity (decibel level).

The adult vervet monkey uses different cries of alarm for different dangers. If the cry warns of a ground-dwelling predator approaching—a leopard or a lion, for example—the monkeys climb the nearest tree. What do they do when they hear the eagle alarm call? They look up, then quickly seek cover in a nearby bush. What if they hear the unique "chatter" that alerts them to a snake? They look down at the ground—then they may actually mob the snake as a group and kill it.

Certain alarm calls make it hard to locate the caller. This makes sense: a caller that leads a predator to it won't last long. But other calls—mating calls, for example—make it easy for the caller to be located, as you might guess. How do monkeys figure out where the caller is? Three cues help: frequency, intensity, and the time the call arrives at each ear. It arrives sooner by a few milliseconds in the ear closer to the sound.

RIGHT-EARED?

Some monkeys listen better with their right ear than their left. Right ear advantage might mean the left half (or hemisphere) of the brain is dominant (stronger). That's the half of the brain that controls language in humans.

Monkeys have different warning calls for different predators. Here, a monkey warns its group of an approaching eagle.

Douc langur, facing page

Seals

(Families: Phocidae and Otariidae)

What happens to a seal's ear when it dives into the water? The channel to its eardrum is closed by water pressure. A pocket of air is trapped inside which acts like a tiny drum, picking up vibrations from the seawater. As a result, seals have excellent underwater hearing. When scientists dangled bells underwater in one experiment, seals immediately came to investigate the noise.

Like dolphins, seals use echolocation to hunt and navigate underwater. Seals give off a series of clicks when they hunt. The clicks then bounce off the fish and lead the seal to its meal. Echolocation works so well that seals can hunt in total darkness.

Seals make other noises besides clicks. They have over thirty underwater calls, each with a different meaning—defending territory, aggression, submission, and mating, to name a few. On land, mother seals and their pups yell and cry at one another across the ice. As the pups grow up, they stop crying, much as human babies learn to talk, and begin to imitate the sounds of the adults around them. Sometimes seals even try to imitate humans. When one folk singer sang a tune called "Seal Song" to a group of seals, one of them "sang" back!

Galapagos fur seal

SEA EARS

Ages ago, some land mammals returned to the sea. At some point on this long evolutionary path, they lost their external ears—a sleek head makes a better swimmer. But sea lions and fur seals kept their outer ears, the only sea mammals to do so. Other evolutionary developments in the aquatic ear include a smaller, thicker eardrum and a very narrow auditory canal. Next time you are in the bath tub, dunk your head under and listen to the water running. Human hearing underwater is pretty good, but not as good as a seal's.

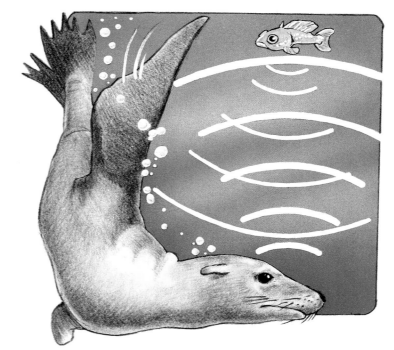

Like dolphins, seals use echolocation to hunt and navigate underwater.

Cape fur seal, facing page

Elephants

African elephant

Elephants really get down with sound—way down. These giant creatures are able to make and hear extremely low-frequency sound, called infrasound. (*Infra* means below.) These sounds are too low for humans to hear. For this reason, elephant behavior has seemed very mysterious to us. For no apparent reason, roaming elephants may suddenly freeze in their tracks and fall silent. Or a group of peaceful elephants at a watering hole may suddenly raise their heads in unison, then stampede off as if their lives depended on it. Until recently, scientists couldn't explain this mysterious behavior. It seemed that elephants communicated through some kind of telepathy, or "mind waves."

Recent experiments using sensitive microphones and recording devices have solved the mystery. Elephants use infrasound to communicate with each other over long distances. They produce these low-frequency calls by vibrating air through their nasal passages past a vocal chord. The vibrating air then travels up to the elephant's forehead, where it vibrates under the skin. These low, rumbling calls can travel as far as $2^{1}/_{2}$ miles, even through thick jungle vegetation that would block higher frequency sounds. In this way, distant groups of elephants can alert each other to the presence of danger or water or food. Though humans can't hear the infrasound calls of elephants, we can sometimes feel the deep vibrations, like distant thunder.

COOL IT

Elephants also use their ears to cool off. Since they have no sweat glands, when they are too hot they hold their ears out away from their heads and flap them slowly back and forth. This cools the blood in the vessels in the ears, which then circulates back to the rest of the body and helps the elephant keep its cool. Lucky for the elephant it has such large ear flaps—the largest in the animal kingdom,

When elephants produce infrasound, their foreheads vibrate.

Elephant, facing page

Owls

(Order: Strigiformes)

Although it has keen vision, an owl can zero in on prey using only its sense of hearing. Even on the darkest nights and at distances as great as half a mile, owls can find the exact location of prey. Owl ears are two long slits on either side of the head, covered by flaps of feathered skin. Owls can move their ear flaps to help them pinpoint the source of a sound. The flaps protect an owl's inner ear and funnel sound into the ear cavity.

Most owls have asymmetrical (uneven) ear cavities located in slightly different positions on either side of their head. Each of the ears works independently. Sounds reach one ear before the other, sending different pieces of information about the prey's location and distance to the owl's brain. The ears of the saw-whet owl are extremely sensitive to sound, but so asymmetrical that this little owl's head looks lopsided!

The process owls use to locate sounds is called triangulation. The "triangle" is formed with the owl's ears as the base angles and the sound source as the third angle. The owl's ears send the information to its brain, which judges the distance and location of a sound source relative to the ears' position. Owls also use their flexible necks to help them fix on the sound source. In fact, they can turn their heads three-quarters of a circle.

Barn owl

FOOLED YOU

An owl's pointy "ear" tufts have nothing at all to do with hearing. They are only showy feathers, called plumage, that stick up on either side of some owls' heads. They were probably misnamed ear tufts because they look like ears.

Owls hear high-frequency sound best, such as the squeak of a mouse—even a half mile away.

Long-eared owl, facing page

Whales

(Order: Cetacea)

A whale's ears appear as two quarter-inch slits on either side of its enormous head. Some scientists believe that whales, like dolphins, use the oil-filled channels in their lower jaws to receive and conduct sound. Whales are mammals, not fish, and their inner ears are very similar to ours (though much bigger!). But their ears have some special features suited to their underwater environment. The middle and inner parts of a whale's ear are set in a rigid, dense bone called the tympanic bulla. This heavy dome helps sound carried through water (which is denser than air) to travel through the auditory canal to the auditory nerves and then to the brain. Whales' large brains are highly developed to interpret sound.

And just what do whales hear in the murky depths? Plenty. Whales produce a wide range of sounds, some of which humans can hear: moans, chirps, grunts, and whale songs. Humpback whales are the opera singers of the deep, able to produce 21 sounds with 84 variations! The sounds are phrases, and each whale seems to put the phrases together differently depending on the message it's sending. Whales can communicate with each other over hundreds of underwater miles. Yet some whale sounds vibrate right past the human ear, too low or too high in frequency to be detected. The very low-frequency sound whales make is called infrasound; the very high-frequency sound is called ultrasound.

Hearing is essential to whales' survival. Since visibility is limited underwater, whales depend on their ears to "see." Like dolphins and seals, they use echolocation to navigate and hunt.

Humpback whale

STRANDED

History has recorded thousands of whale strandings on beaches. Until recently, however, the reason for this was a mystery. Now, some cetologists (scientists who study whales) believe that whales beach themselves when their echolocation system is disrupted. Shallow, muddy waters or sudden changes in the Earth's magnetic field can confuse a whale's ability to echolocate with accuracy.

Why do whales beach themselves? Probably because their echolocation system has been "jammed."

Orca, facing page

HUMans

(Homo sapiens)

What do you hear at this very moment? Whatever sounds you hear are traveling on waves of air. Sound waves hit your outer ears (pinnae) first, the fleshy, boneless half-circles on either side of your head. The shape of the pinna funnels the sounds toward the hole in the middle of your ear. This is the opening of the auditory canal. The sound wave travels down the canal and, at the end, beats on the eardrum. The eardrum is delicate and easily damaged.

The vibration of the eardrum passes the sound into the middle ear. The middle ear has three of the smallest bones in your body. Named after their shapes, they are the hammer, the anvil, and the stirrup. These bones vibrate and pass the sound to the inner ear. There, the sound enters a very small organ that looks like a snail shell, called the cochlea. Inside the cochlea, sensitive hair-like cells brush against the end of auditory nerve. This nerve changes the sound wave into a signal called a nerve impulse. This causes the *sensation* of hearing, but not yet the *perception* (understanding). The impulse then travels to your brain, which understands the impulse as sound and usually recognizes what the sound is—laughter, for example.

An organ as important and sensitive as your ear needs protection. Lined with tiny hairs, your ear canal "sweats" a sticky earwax called cerumen. The hairs and the earwax catch dust and other particles and prevent insects from wandering into your ear and causing trouble.

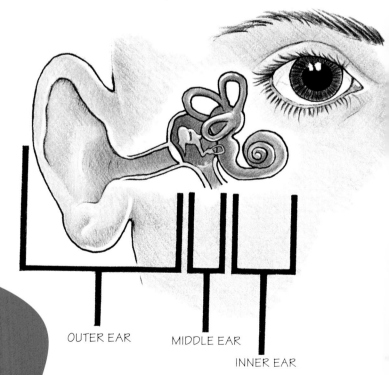

OUTER EAR   MIDDLE EAR
INNER EAR

The human ear extends far into the skull— beneath your eyeballs, in fact.

EAR POPPING

A passage called the Eustachian tube leads from the ear to the throat. It helps to keep the air pressure in the middle ear the same as the air pressure outside the ear. When we change altitude—for example, driving up in the mountains or flying in an airplane—our sense of hearing is temporarily impaired until our ears "pop" and the air pressure is equalized again.

44

GLOSSARIZED INDEX

This glossarized index will help you find specific information about the sense of hearing. will also help you understand the meaning of some of the words used in this book.

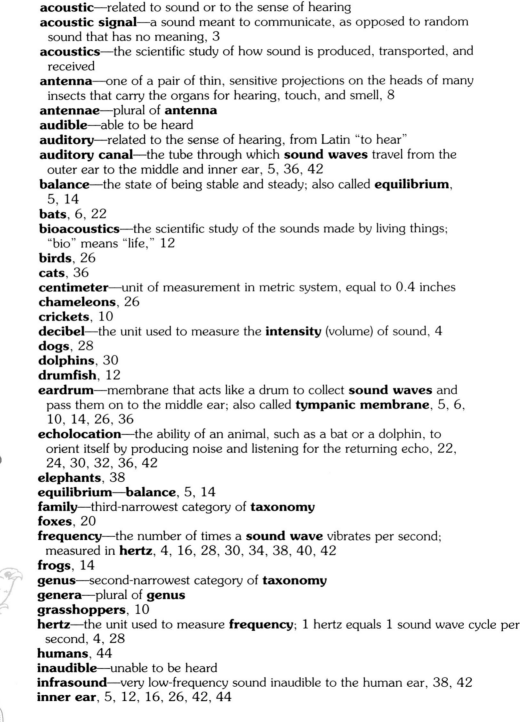

Other books about animals and the five senses:

Amazing Animal Senses, Ron Van Der Meer, Little, Brown & Company, 1990, 0-316-89624-1

Animal Senses, Jim Flegg, Newington Press, 1991, 1-878137-21-2

Extraordinary Eyes: How Animals See the World, Sandra Sinclair, R.R. Bowker, 1991, 0-8037-0806-8

Fingers & Feelers, Henry Pluckrose, Watts, Franklin, Incorporated, 1990, 0-531-14050-4

Tongues & Tasters, Henry Pluckrose, Watts, Franklin, Incorporated, 1990, 0-531-14049-0

Touch, Taste & Smell, Steve Parker, Watts, Franklin, Incorporated, 1989, 0-531-10655-1

Why Do Cats' Eyes Glow in the Dark?: (And Other Questions Kids Ask about Animals), Joanne Settel & Nancy Baggett, Atheneum-MacMillan, 1988, 0-689-31267-9

Photo credits:

BIZARRE & BEAUTIFUL SERIES

A spirited and fun investigation of the mysteries of the five senses in the animal kingdom.

Each title is 8½" x 11", 48 pages, $14.95 hardcover, with color photographs and illustrations throughout.

Bizarre & Beautiful Ears (available 9/93)
Bizarre & Beautiful Eyes (available 9/93)
Bizarre & Beautiful Feelers (available 10/93)
Bizarre & Beautiful Noses (available 9/93)
Bizarre & Beautiful Tongues (available 11/93)

RAINBOW WARRIOR ARTISTS SERIES

W hat is a Rainbow Warrior Artist? It is a person who strives to live in harmony with the Earth and all living creatures, and who tries to better the world while living his or her life in a creative way.

Each title is written by Reavis Moore with a foreword by LeVar Burton, and is 8½" x 11", 48 pages, $14.95 hardcover, with color photographs and illustrations.

Native Artists of Africa (available 1/94)
Native Artists of North America

ROUGH AND READY SERIES

L earn about the men and women who settled the American frontier. Explore the myths and legends about these coura-geous individuals and learn about the environmental, cultural, and economic legacies they left to us.

Each title is written by A. S. Gintzler and is 48 pages, 8½" x 11", $12.95 hardcover, with two-color illustrations and duotone archival photographs.

Rough and Ready Cowboys (available 4/94)
Rough and Ready Homesteaders (available 4/94)
Rough and Ready Prospectors (available 4/94)

AMERICAN ORIGINS SERIES

M any of us are the third and fourth generation of our families to live in America. Learn what our great-great grandparents experienced when they arrived here and how much of our lives are still intertwined with theirs.

Each title is 48 pages, 8½" x 11", $12.95 hardcover, with two-color illustrations and duotone archival photographs.

Tracing Our German Roots, Leda Silver (available 12/93)
Tracing Our Irish Roots, Sharon Moscinski (available 10/93)
Tracing Our Italian Roots, Kathleen Lee (available 10/93)
Tracing Our Jewish Roots, Miriam Sagan (available 12/93)

EXTREMELY WEIRD SERIES

All of the titles are written by Sarah Lovett, 8¹/₂" x 11", 48 pages, $9.95 paperbacks, with color photographs and illustrations.

Extremely Weird Bats
Extremely Weird Birds
Extremely Weird Endangered Species
Extremely Weird Fishes
Extremely Weird Frogs
Extremely Weird Insects
Extremely Weird Mammals (available 8/93)
Extremely Weird Micro Monsters (available 8/93)
Extremely Weird Primates
Extremely Weird Reptiles
Extremely Weird Sea Creatures
Extremely Weird Snakes (available 8/93)
Extremely Weird Spiders

X-RAY VISION SERIES

Each title in the series is 8¹/₂" x 11", 48 pages, $9.95 paperback, with color photographs and illustrations and written by Ron Schultz.

Looking Inside the Brain
Looking Inside Cartoon Animation
Looking Inside Caves and Caverns
 (available 11/93)
Looking Inside Sports Aerodynamics
Looking Inside Sunken Treasure
Looking Inside Telescopes and the Night Sky

THE KIDDING AROUND TRAVEL GUIDES

All of the titles listed below are 64 pages and $9.95 paperbacks, except for *Kidding Around the National Parks* and *Kidding Around Spain*, which are 108 pages and $12.95 paperbacks.

Kidding Around Atlanta
Kidding Around Boston, 2nd ed.
Kidding Around Chicago, 2nd ed.
Kidding Around the Hawaiian Islands
Kidding Around London
Kidding Around Los Angeles
Kidding Around the National Parks
 of the Southwest
Kidding Around New York City, 2nd ed.
Kidding Around Paris
Kidding Around Philadelphia
Kidding Around San Diego
Kidding Around San Francisco
Kidding Around Santa Fe
Kidding Around Seattle
Kidding Around Spain
Kidding Around Washington, D.C., 2nd ed.

MASTERS OF MOTION SERIES

Each title in the series is 10¹/₄" x 9", 48 pages, $9.95 paperback, with color photographs and illustrations.

How to Drive an Indy Race Car
 David Rubel
How to Fly a 747
 Tim Paulson
How to Fly the Space Shuttle
 Russell Shorto

THE KIDS EXPLORE AMERICA SERIES

Each title is written by kids for kids by the Westridge Young Writers Workshop, 7" x 9", with photographs and illustrations by the kids.

Kids Explore America's Hispanic Heritage
112 pages, $7.95 paper
Kids Explore America's African-American Heritage
128 pages, $8.95 paper
Kids Explore the Gifts of Children with Special Needs
112 pages, $8.95 paper (available 2/94)
Kids Explore America's Japanese Heritage
112 pages, $8.95 paper (available 4/94)

ENVIRONMENTAL TITLES

Habitats: Where the Wild Things Live
Randi Hacker and Jackie Kaufman
8¹/₂" x 11", 48 pages, color illustrations, $9.95 paper

The Indian Way: Learning to Communicate with Mother Earth
Gary McLain
7" x 9", 114 pages, illustrations, $9.95 paper

Rads, Ergs, and Cheeseburgers:
The Kids' Guide to Energy and the Environment
Bill Yanda
7" x 9", 108 pages, two-color illustrations, $13.95 paper

The Kids' Environment Book:
What's Awry and Why
Anne Pedersen
7" x 9", 192 pages, two-color illustrations, $13.95 paper